Nathan Coppedge

PSYCHOLOGICAL

KNOWLEDGE

Nathan Coppedge

Nathan Coppedge

What Wisdom Do I Have That Others Don't Have?:

Perhaps most of my insights that really seemed like insights relate to exceptions in reality.

In the wisdom department, I know that it is usually the very beginning of a thought process that can lead someone down the wrong path. A lot of people don't seem to question their assumptions, or feel satisfied accepting some degree of imperfection in their past. Even though perfectionism runs the risk of stress and madness, its one of the best ways to pursue the best life.

Once we accept perfectionism, many choices are more arbitrary than we think. The stress we bear from day to day is sometimes an arbitrary choice based on what we merely ASSUME is appropriate. We can feel better by training ourselves to be patient, and make slow turns towards a healthier mentality. For example, it is possible to become vegetarian, to avoid depression, or to be more intellectual. However, these options imply changing more than one thing about one's life simultaneously.

At the root of it, what inspires us is the least flexible thing. If we can change what inspires us, we have the ability to change everything about ourselves.

Collectively, these 'secrets' are very powerful for creating change in one's life.

Nathan Coppedge

Advanced Concept of Development

Organization of levels is something of a difficult task, since many beings see themselves in
different ways.

I have already given the organization of 'the
levels of path' in the following form: (1) Brute
Survival. (2) Organized Warfare. (3) Economic
Value. (4) Intellectual Meaning.

That is more of a historical perspective than an
objective view.

An initial guide to objective levels may be
found by the following organization:

1. The Trivial. Mere opinions. Arbitrary judg-
ments. Confusion. Lack of reality. Requires a
basic paradigm and no work.

2. The Real. That which makes an impression,
and little more. That which can be counted on.
The conventional. The predictable. The things
that do not always require knowledge. Requires a basic paradigm and work.

3. The Dimensional. The conceptual and mean-
ingful. That which understands the real. It requires an advanced paradigm AND work.

4. The Ideal. That which has extended beyond reality into hyper-reality and fantasy. That which no longer requires a conventional standard. That which requires an advanced paradigm, but no work.

We can see from these four fundamental levels THAT leveling involves advancement under two paradigms: (1) Actualization, and (2) Meaning. Moving beyond actualized meaning would mean extending beyond the first MAJOR quadra of levels. Doing so reliably would not be easy, but may be possible.

PSYCHOLOGICAL SYSTEMS

INFANTILE PSYCHOLOGY

Infants, it is known, have a lot of care for their mothers.

Much of the infant's immediate life has to do with his or her

dependence on the mother.

The infant may also learn a lot from the mother's and father's

response to him or her, and the initial ex-periences in the hospital

or wherever else the infant is born.

Indeed, the child's early experiences are exaggerated. Depending

on what senses are available to the child, the infant may learn considerably, or else not as much as aver-age.

The earliest experiences are the moments in which the infant

reaches the first inclinations towards what-ever wisdom or insight

that will be had later in life.

This first insight has two parts: (1) The child's unhindered

perceptions about the world, whether pleasant or unpleasant,

whether insightful, or recoiling, etc. and (2) The permission

granted throughout later life to trust these perceptions and enjoy

or critique existence.

The first major opportunity for the infant may be to avoid

suffering, and if this is not successful the world becomes a

treacherous place, full of shadows and phantoms.

The second opportunity is to be wise, and this is on the basis of

the extent to which the infant's first insights can blossom. That is,

whether the infant was confused or not. How fresh in memory,

how free of narcotics was the mother, etc.

The third opportunity is to be critical, which is something that

tends to happen to a greater extent if the child is unhappy, but

also when the child is supported by the en-vironment.

Thus, the Happy, Wise, and Petulent chil-dren are the three

archetypes that emerge. And their semi-forms are respetively the

Funny, Intelligent, and Perceptive.

The best to emerge from a bad life is the perceptive child, while

the best to emerge from a good life is the happy child. In that

way, there is some compensation for the pains of life.

PSYCHO-ANALYTIC SYSTEMS

MAINSTREAM PSYCHOLOGY

Mainstream psychology has a reputation for a certain nimble,

affable attitude which makes its subjects more appealing to a

popular audience. This form of psychology is virtually unique for

its 1-to-1 relevance to the audience, and its immediate

applicability in the personal and inter-personal world of its

audience.

Mainstream psychology is often summa-rized in individual 'grand

theses', often combining words such as 'individual (adj.)',

'passivity / aggression / intelligence /

schizophrenia / depression',

'improves / spirals out of control', 'under some [stated] conditions'.

The conditions can be stated to be a by-product of further factors

such as 'de-socialization / de-sensitization / stimulation / group

settings'. Some bizarre theses seem to hold under the conditions

of certain illnesses, or under bizarre stimulus. Thus, some of the

conditions may have results only under 'over-exposure / with high

intensity' or 'if the client is sensitive to the stimulus'.

Thus, mainstream psychology can be mapped as follows:

1. Sensitive?

2. Exposed?

3. Bizarre?

4. Social psychology?

5. Stimulus? De-sensitized or de-socialized?

6. Condition?

7. Chronic?

8. Depressed?

9. Dysfunctional?

10. Intelligent (specific sensitivity)?

11. Passive / aggressive (hidden symptoms)?

For example,

A. Bee-sting. Physical sensitivity. Requires physical treatment or

tolerance.

B. Allergy to yogurt. Sensitivity with a condition. May affect

certain social situations.

C. Person is behaving bizarrely because they are not wearing any

clothes. Person may have dementia or excessive promiscuity.

Problem needs to be solved immediately.

D. Person feels social anxiety. Person is otherwise mentally

healthy. Condition which applies in all social situations.

E. Person has a concealed megalomania. This is social

psychology that applies only in certain social situations.

F. Person is feeling discomfort in the office. This may be a

product of a physical or mental condition.

G. Person is feeling very alert. The person may be drugged or

experiencing psychosis or exaggerated emotions.

H. Person doesn't show up at the appointment. Person may be

disorganized, forgetful, or have a physical impairment.

I. Person's condition doesn't improve. The condition may be

habitual, chronic, fatal, or in some other way serious.

J. Person is dysfunctional and blames their mood. Person may be

depressed.

K. Person doesn't handle social situations very well. Person may

be emotionally immature, abused, schizo-phrenic, or

developmentally abnormal (high I.Q.).

L. Person is especially complex on one issue. Person may simply

have special knowledge in this area (high I.Q.).

M. Person is especially un-forthcoming on one particular topic in

her life. Person may have suppressed memories.

PSYCHO-ANALYTIC SYSTEMS

HARMONIZING

There is much confusion about the con-
cept of harmonization. It

has been seen as central to functional psychology for a long time.

However, its root causes, and the means
of sustaining it have

been (for some) by turns difficult or ob-
scure.

Harmonizing, which is the process of
reaching harmonization,

comes about through a practical focus on
positive thinking, both

to avoid disaster, and to promote valuable
mentalistic vibes.

Harmonization becomes more difficult for

those who are

brain-damaged, or for some other reason
cannot find genuine

mental stimulation. The ability to stimulate
the mind is what

separates so-called 'ordinary' people from
those who are

considered abnormal. Further traits such
as ethical conduct,

professional qualifications, fatherliness or
motherliness, etc.

seperate further the functional types, but
for dysfunctional people

some or all of these additional traits may
often be impossible.

Harmonization becomes the exclusive
bridge between functional

and dysfunctional people, and it is by no
means an easy bridge to

cross, as the positive elements of harmony
are held almost

exclusively by functional people.

A key element to understand is that harmonizing involves

ignoring and eliminating harmful vibes,
which can be detected and

criticized by those with intellectual sensitivity. The truly

functional people tend to be high intellectual performers, or at

least high social performers.

On the converse, ignoring harmful vibes
has been critiqued as a

'following-the-herd' mentality, but so long
as mental stimulation

is a desirable end in itself, some degree of
conformism is largely

unavoidable, and can even inspire envy.

Intellectual sensitivity and higher cognitive

traits become the

defense against invasive negative behav-
iors that could

compromise the culture and chemistry of
such close-knit

networks of reward and response.

The reward, some say it is a lofty one, is to
be mentally

constructive by providing a culture for the
higher mental

ambitions of groups of individuals. Because groups tend to have

higher social functions than individuals,
there is an advantage in

giving preference to group function over
individual function.

On the other hand, ignoring individual
function may prohibit

creativity if the focus is no longer on genuine individual

accomplishment. Thus, the model must be accepted on a chemical

level of mutual exchange before harmonization works for

individuals.

It is then likely that the system of harmonization is keyed into

patterns that only emerge with sexual or narcotic stimulus.

So, while harmony works for society, it is superficial in the sense

that it has no one individual's interest in mind independent of the

overall social function.

On the other hand, it is geared towards the immediate chemical

achievement of every individual in the context of any existing context of limitations.

Harmony thus involves such things as sim-
ple awareness, the

desire for stimulus, and social priorities
which are assumed to be

the honest traits of humans as individuals
when they seek to fulfill

non-negativist priorities.

PSYCHO-ANALYTIC SYSTEMS

INDIVIDUATION

INSPIRATION --- At first, the individual (subject) is surrounded

by talented people, often people who play music instruments.

Their talent is explained by the fact that they have already

individuated. This is also the time when the person first hears the

word 'individual'.

THE LIE --- The person sees that there is something wrong with

the world. The person struggles and is taken down by a

psychological or physical condition of some type. He or she hears

the word 'individuation' if it is psychological, or 'habit' /

'habitation' / 'habituation' if it is physical. The physical response

leads to questions such as, is it worth it to spend time, is life worth

it, is the physical world inspiring, etc. It cannot be argued that

both worlds are equally interesting, so the physical answer may

involve some sort of artificial death or historical lapse into the

psychological condition. In effect, the physical model becomes the

background.

THEORY AND PROOF --- The individual explores creativity or

whatever else he or she feels like doing. The result is a theory

(what he or she is doing) and confirmation (proof of the theory),

not to be confused with the later stage.

IMMERSION OR DENIAL ---- As life becomes more like a

mental construct that responds to some of the person's thoughts

(e.g. the person gets some of what is wanted), either the person

immerses him or herself in pleasures, or he or she denies him or

herself some of the pleasures. The result is two different

personalities, one finding unreality in the physical body, and the

other finding unreality in the mind.

CONFORMATION --- The theory, whether it is flesh or mind,

becomes all-important, and the persons' beliefs as they become

more sophisticated are also confirmed or supported.

ELEVATION - THE KISS ---- Rewards become immaterial or

else confirm one's habituation in the world. One enters 'the psychological cocoon'.

Nathan Coppedge

PSYCHO-ANALYTIC SYSTEMS

GESTALT THEORY

Take a value and find out that it's true, and theoretically you've

found what is known as a 'gestalt' or deep psychological truism.

For example, if authentic life is happy, and happiness is always

symbolized by the color 'yellow', then we can say 'life is yellow'

is a gestalt. Even if it isn't 100% true, it is a truism because its

supposed to be true.

Similarly, we can say 'systems live in trees' if all systems come

from linear structures which are called trees.

26

PSYCHO-ANALYTIC SYSTEMS

MNEMOSIS

Mnemosis, or recovery of memories, is a technique that has

fallen out of fashion in psychology. Psychologists have discovered

that patients are dishonest, temperamental, or just can't get

themselves to remember everything.

Nonetheless, confrontation with past events is an important

process in therapy, and takes place even if it is not frankly

acknowledged. And, often the therapist is aware of this.

The process may vary somewhat, but it is usually in the following form:

1. The therapist asks the patient polite
questions (how he or she

is feeling, what is something that matters
to them, where have

they traveled to, etc.)

2. The therapist asks the patient to explain
something in their life

that is important to them, such as a memory that they think of

fondly, or some recent experience that has
troubled them.

3. Instead of immediately analyzing what
the trouble or

significance means, the therapist asks the
person what the thing,

event, significance, etc. means to the patient.

4. Through internally analyzing what the patient interprets from

the experience, the therapist begins to understand the patient.

5. The therapist can develop a network of associations about the

patient by asking more questions, and delving deeper into the

patient's past experiences and associations.

6. Finally, through guidance from the therapist, the patient is led

into an understanding of what is most important to them.

7. If what seems most important is something harmful or

dangerous, the therapist can warn the patient that there is

something harmful or dangerous lurking in their psyche.

APPLIED SYSTEMS

BRAIN REPAIR

POODLE EFFECT:

This is something I have noticed that is
very important, so I will

mention it first.

People are often set off course by the ap-
pearance of poodles!

Seriously!

They think their brain is composed like a
poodle, and then they

have to undo the effect!

Until they learn to squash in these exaggerated 'puffs' of their

brain, there is no hope of recovering mental function.

This effect is even more extreme on the brain than the

hyper-activity resulting from sugar, only the effect is opposite.

Overcoming the poodle effect could almost be called the first

stage towards mental functionality. But we should ultimately

avoid expressions like 'ascendent brain' as these may have

similar effects, albeit not as extreme as the poodle.

I have cured at least one person's thought-lessness by mentioning

this problem!

Ignorance-Denial:

Are you imagining the obvious when you need to?

Are your eyes black and you have never thought they could be

like charcoal, even in passing?

This may be a sign of excessive mental restraint.

Instead, consider the obvious, and reject it if you like.

The process can be oft-repeated.

MISCELLANEOUS INSIGHTS

The opti-mystics thought wine was blood and wasn't for drinking. The pessi-mystics thought wine was poison and drunk it up.

I have found those accepting illusions are those forgiving god, whereas pleasure is simply the pursuit of genius.

Surely one doesn't need a lifetime for every lesson! Most life-lessons seem to amount to this.

'Practical' is the most ideal word in a higher language.

Things are as valuable as they are,
But they are not as valuable as we assume!

When we have the best senses, there is no pain. We have to balance who we are relative to what we observe, that's what creates pain.

Humans are infinitely sensitive, but not ab-
solutely.

Faith in pain is meaningless.

Nathan Coppedge

I think possibly each life has a different
metaphysical existence, and sometimes
these metaphysical existences are held in
common with other people When they are
held in common with other people, then
they have a political reality, or an economic reality, or a divine reality, etc. Different labels might apply in different
'universes' although some of the universes
are really earlier or later variations of other
universes, and sometimes even things like
'Time' might exist in one universe but not
in another. The conditions of the universe
depend both on the big and the small, and
people can think that small or big things
matter almost arbitrarily, deciding how life
is determined for themselves (if they have
authority), and for something else outside
themselves if they do not have authority.
And this intuition might only apply to some
small aspect of the real reality.

CAN JUNG'S ARCHETPES BE FALSI-
FIED?

Principles from Gestalt Theory have
some appeal, such as the idea that
'all systems are up a tree' because a
linear structure prefigures many system structures. Or, the idea that
'nature is yellow' if yellow represents
happiness, and happiness is optimal,
and nature is ideally optimal. These
ideas are idealistic to be sure, but
higher cognition does not necessarily
eliminate idealistic notions, and may
often gain usefulness by placing de-
mands on them.

There is a big difference between
Jung's archetypes conceived in an
obvious sense, say, interpolated with
media images or memes, and Jung's
archetypes seen in great depth. I
think the moral of the archetypes is
that (1) They or incoherent, because
one image is not compatible with another, etc. or (2) They are coherent,
but only insofar as they meet the cri-
teria of coherency. With this understanding, it is possible to examine
the archetypes carefully and extract
a psychological lesson focusing on
voluntary self-development. I think
this is the core lesson that Jung
meant to protract.

RECOMMENDED READING

The Dimensional Psychologist's Toolkit

The Dimensional Encyclopedia

Psychological Knowledge

Nathan Coppedge

Psychological Knowledge

NATHAN COPPEDGE is the author of numerous books on psychology, including titles on child development, mental-health focus, and traditional psychology. The present work is a compilation of previous writings including those included in Systems Theory, a larger work by the same author.

www.ingramcontent.com/pod-product-compliance
Lightning Source LLC
Chambersburg PA
CBHW061928280526
45787CB00004B/1531